E.T.

THE EXTRA-TERRESTRIAL

DISCOVERS
Plants

Simon Smiley

KINGFISHER/UNIVERSAL
Kingfisher Publications Plc
New Penderel House
283-288 High Holborn
London WC1V 7HZ
www.kingfisherpub.com

First published by Kingfisher Publications Plc in 2002

10 9 8 7 6 5 4 3 2 1

1TR/1201/TWP/MAR(MAR)/130SINAR

A CIP catalogue for this book is available from the British Library.

ISBN 0 7534 0733 7

Printed in Singapore

Author: Simon Smiley
 Project Manager: Belinda Weber
  Editor: Christine Hatt
   Art Editor: Eljay Yildirim
    Designer: Dean Price
     DTP Manager: Nicky Studdart
      Production Controller: Debbie Otter,
       Kelly Johnson

Contents

World of Plants   4

How Do Plants Grow?   6

Flowering Plants   8

Fruits and Seeds   10

Trees and Forests   12

Weird Plants   14

Dry Desert Plants   16

Wet, Weedy World   18

Fantastic Fungi   20

Plant Defences   22

Growing Great Plants   24

Plants for Food and Healing   26

Useful Plants   28

Going Home   30

World of Plants

Plants are amazing, living, green machines! They take in sunlight and drink water. They make things that we need, such as food, wood and the oxygen gas in the air we breathe. E.T. has learned that about 300,000 kinds of plants grow on the Earth.

Plants on a stick

The giants of the plant world are trees. We use their tough, wooden trunks for building and for fuel. The world's tallest trees are redwoods like this. They grow in the USA.

Soft, spongy mosses grow everywhere except in the sea. You will even find them where it is too cold or dry for other plants to survive. Some live around the frosty South Pole.

Beautiful plants

Most plants have flowers, but not all flowers have bright colours and smell sweet. Some are so tiny and dull that you have to look hard to find them.

PHONE HOME FACTS

The cycad palms of South Africa and Australia are the oldest kind of seed-making plants. 200 million years ago, dinosaurs lurked in lush cycad forests.

Ferns grow well in damp places. Their leaves, called fronds, uncurl as they grow. Ferns are among the oldest plants. About 300 million years ago, ferns as big as trees grew in great forests.

INFORMATION OVERLOAD!

E.T. has collected so many fascinating facts that he must send them back to his planet to be analysed.

Trees live much longer than many other plants. Some bristlecone pine trees alive today sprouted from seeds 5,000 years ago.

More plants grow in rainforests than anywhere else. In an area the size of a small town, there may be 750 different trees and 1,500 other types of plant.

Plants grow almost everywhere. But they cannot survive in total darkness, for example in caves or deep oceans.

How Do Plants Grow?

Plants are greedy eaters. They guzzle air, light and water so that they can grow fast and make more plants. A green chemical makes the plants' food from air, light and water where it is needed most – in the plants' leaves.

Plant-making

Plants have clever ways of making new plants. Some plants grow from bits that break away from bigger plants. Plants that flower make seeds from which more plants grow.

A new plant could grow from every one of these water melon seeds.

If you break a leaf off a jade plant, then put it in watered soil, a new plant will grow. Here, three new plants are busily growing.

Looking at leaves

Leaves are covered in tiny holes. Through these 'mouths', plants breathe in air. Water can escape through the holes. So when the soil is dry, the leaves close them.

Green food factory

Plants need water, air and light to grow. Follow the labels round clockwise to see how plants take in these three things – and what they make with them.

The plant 'factory' also makes oxygen. It comes out of the leaves into the air.

Sunlight gives energy to a green chemical in leaves called chlorophyll.

The food flows around the plant as a liquid called sap.

Leaves also take in a gas called carbon dioxide from the air.

From the Sun energy, gas and water, chlorophyll in leaves makes sugary plant food.

Roots suck up water and minerals (chemicals) from the soil.

INFORMATION OVERLOAD!

E.T. has collected so many fascinating facts that he must send them back to his planet to be analysed.

Bamboo plants hold the growth speed record. They zoom upwards at nearly 4 centimetres an hour.

Some rainforest vines suck water up from their roots at 0.4 metres a second. So they can carry water up to the tree tops in five minutes.

Sunflower heads grow unevenly – first one side grows fast, then the other. This makes the heads continually turn to face the Sun as they grow.

Flowering Plants

Flowers smell great and their colours brighten our lives. But flowers do not put on this show for humans (or E.T.)! They do it to attract insects. Without visits from insects, few flowers would make seeds from which new plants could grow in the spring.

Pollen exchange

Plants are made from tiny building blocks called cells. Flowers make male and female cells. A powder called pollen contains the male cells. The pollen sticks to visiting insects, and they carry it to other flowers. With the pollen, the female parts of the other flowers make seeds.

POLLEN-COVERED STAMENS

Flower parts called stamens make pollen. Insects cannot help brushing against the stamens of this lily and carrying away the pollen dust.

Attracting insects

Flowers attract insects with their colour and smell. And they reward visiting insects with a drink of nectar, a sweet juice. To reach the nectar, insects squeeze past the flowers' male and female parts. They spread pollen on the way.

A bee spreads pollen to a clover flower.

EARTH ALERT!

Wild flowers are pretty, but you should not pick them. This is because some are rare. If you pick them, they will not be able to make seeds to grow more flowers.

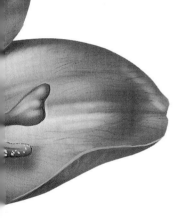

A big family!

There are about 250,000 types of flowering plant – more than of any other kind. The biggest members of the flowering plant family are trees, such as this cherry.

INFORMATION OVERLOAD!

E.T. has collected so many fascinating facts that he must send them back to his planet to be analysed.

Pollen grains are tiny. 3,000 of them would easily fit on the head of a pin.

Breathing in tiny pollen grains gives some people sneezing, eye-watering hay fever.

Bees turn the nectar that they collect into honey. To make one teaspoonful, they must fly an average of 175 kilometres.

Fruits and Seeds

E.T. has learned that fruits are the hitch-hikers of the plant world. After animals eat fruits, they carry the seeds inside far from where the fruits grew. The seeds come out in the animals' droppings and new plants grow from them.

BRAZIL NUT

Nuts are fruits with a hard case. You need to crack them open to get at the single seed inside.

How many seeds?

Some fruits, such as water melons, have many small seeds. But stone fruits, such as peaches, have one big seed.

PHONE HOME FACTS

Never stand under a double coconut palm! Its seeds are the biggest of any plant. They weigh up to 27 kilograms – as much as a television set.

BEAN SEED

ROOT

Plant a bean in an earth-filled jar, then watch it sprout and grow.

Not all plants use fruits to spread their seeds. Sycamore seeds use their 'rotors' to make spinning flights far from the trees they grew on.

Birds that pluck dates like these may drop the seeds in them many kilometres away.

All you need – in a seed

A seed contains all that is needed to make a new plant, even food. When the seed is wet and warm enough, it sprouts. A tiny root grows down, while a tiny shoot grows up.

BEAN PLANT

SHOOT

Trees and Forests

Trees are the tallest plants. In wild forests, these green giants provide homes and food for millions of creatures. Trees are valuable to people and E.T. We make buildings and paper from their woody trunks. And we breathe in the oxygen gas made in their leaves.

Trees such as pines have green, needle-like leaves. They stay on all year, so the trees are known as evergreens. In places with cool winters, the leaves of broadleaf trees go brown and fall off in the autumn.

Flat, wide leaves grow on the branches of trees such as oaks. That is why they are called broadleaf trees.

EARTH ALERT!

Tropical forests are shrinking as people cut down trees for their wood. Unless we look after these forests better, the rare plants and animals in them will die out.

Fabulous forests

When trees cover large areas, they form forests. Tropical forests grow in a band around the Earth's middle called the Equator. More types of animals and plants live here than anywhere else on the Earth.

Japanese bonsai are perfect miniature trees. Gardeners keep them small by cutting the roots and branches.

Weird Plants

Sticky sundews and smelly rafflesias are two of the weird plants that E.T. has seen growing on the Earth. If he looks very carefully, he'll find many more.

Insects cannot grip the shiny insides of the pitcher plant. So they slide down into a pool of liquid. Then their bodies rot and feed the plant.

Gigantic grasses

Bamboo is a kind of woody grass. Some types grow an amazing 4 centimetres an hour, up to a height of 40 metres. That's as high as a ten-storey building. Others produce flowers just once every 120 years!

PHONE HOME FACTS

The vast leaf of the giant water lily can measure nearly two metres from side to side, making it as big as a dinner table. The lily grows in the waters of one of the world's longest rivers, the Amazon of South America.

The hot-lips plant has two leaves that look just like a big red mouth! It grows in the Caribbean.

Shiny droplets on the leaves of the sundew attract insects. Once the insects have landed, the plant's sticky hairs stop them escaping.

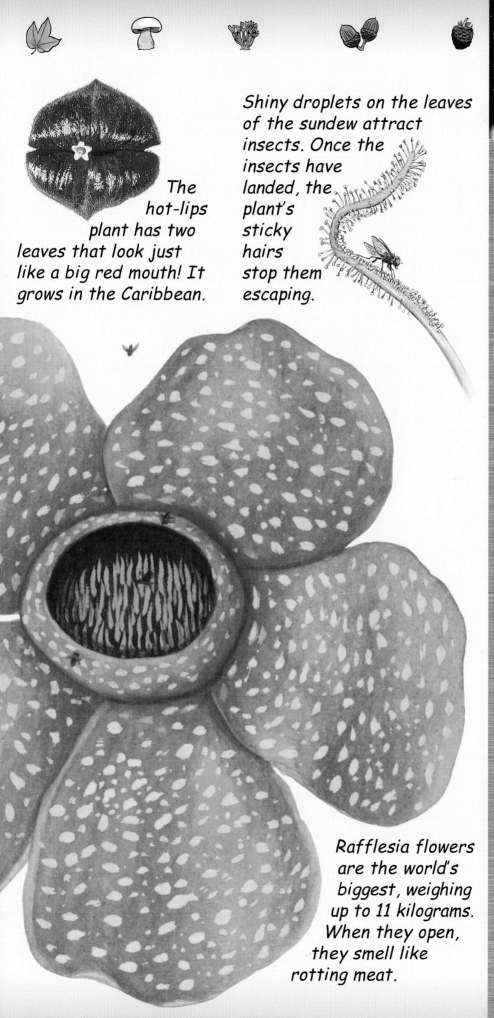

Rafflesia flowers are the world's biggest, weighing up to 11 kilograms. When they open, they smell like rotting meat.

INFORMATION OVERLOAD!

E.T. has collected so many fascinating facts that he must send them back to his planet to be analysed.

The saguaro of North America is the world's largest cactus. One plant can weigh nine tonnes.

The Venus flytrap's leaves have a hinge. When flies land on a leaf, the hinge shuts, trapping the fly inside.

The baobab tree of Australia and Africa stores water in its trunk. This makes the trunk lumpy. When the weather is dry, the tree uses the water and the trunk gets flatter.

Dry Desert Plants

E.T. knows he should never ask a cactus for a drink! These spiky plants grow in deserts, the driest places in the world. They survive by collecting water from the air and the soil. And by never, ever, giving water to strangers.

A 12-metre spike carries the century plant's blooms. It flowers just once, after growing for 10 to 15 years.

'Living stones', also called pebble plants, save water and energy by growing only in the cooler seasons. The summer's heat slows or stops their growth.

Bats help some desert plants to spread pollen. The bats pick up pollen on their fur when they visit the flowers at night to drink nectar.

EARTH ALERT!

Travellers once cut down cacti to suck water from them. This can kill 100-year-old plants. So if you visit a desert, take plenty of water!

Storing water

Desert plants keep a water supply in their big roots, their fat stems, or their fleshy leaves. Some also have a layer of fine hairs that traps air. The air stops the plants from drying out.

INFORMATION OVERLOAD!

E.T. has collected so many fascinating facts that he must send them back to his planet to be analysed.

A single large cactus can store enough water to fill 300 buckets.

Not all cactuses contain water that you can drink. Water from some of them, such as the saguaro cactus, contains poison.

If the desert soil gets wet, plants in it quickly grow more roots to suck up the extra water.

Wet, Weedy World

E.T. knows that not all plants grow on land. Water weed lives in ponds and rivers. Seaweed grows on shores. Plankton float out at sea. These plants help keep water fresh and are food for water creatures.

Seaweed floats everywhere in the Sargasso Sea, part of the Atlantic Ocean. In the days of sailing ships, sailors worried that they would get tangled up in the weed.

Strong seaweed

Most seaweeds grow like floating forests in shallow water. Their strong stems grip the rocks. Their leaves may be twice as long as an ocean-racing yacht.

Pond garden

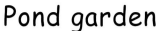

Many pond and river plants float at the surface of water. Blanket weed forms slimy mats. Duckweed is the world's smallest flowering plant. Lilies have round leaves and big, beautiful flowers.

The smallest ocean plants are called plankton. One teaspoon of ocean water contains a million of them. Tiny sea creatures eat the plankton. Small fish eat the tiny sea creatures. And big fish eat the smaller fish. So all ocean life depends on plankton.

PHONE HOME FACTS

Astronauts plan to take plankton on long space journeys as food. As they grow, the plants will take in harmful gases, keeping the spacecraft air fresh. E.T. should get some plankton for his trip home!

INFORMATION OVERLOAD!

E.T. has collected so many fascinating facts that he must send them back to his planet to be analysed.

Plankton keep the world's air fresh. If all the plankton died, poisonous gases would quickly kill all humans and animals on the Earth.

Blankets of weed growing in shallow seawater help to protect the shore from the waves crashing on to it.

Some tiny plant plankton are hard to tell from animals. They swim by lashing their tiny tails, and can eat particles of food.

Fantastic Fungi

They make bread rise. They grow between your toes. They are delicious foods – or deadly poisons. Fungi are all these things and more. The mushrooms E.T. likes to eat are a type of fungi. So are toadstools, yeasts and moulds.

This death cap is among the deadliest of fungi.

The moulds that grow on old foods are tiny, thread-shaped fungi. Thousands of fungi growing close together create the coloured, furry patches.

Fly agaric
Strong poisons in the fly agaric mushroom give people who eat the fungus scary dreams and visions.

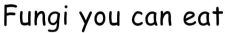

Fungi you can eat

Many fungi are delicious to eat. You can buy mushrooms like these at lots of shops, because they are easy to farm. The mushrooms grow on horse manure in damp places such as cellars or caves.

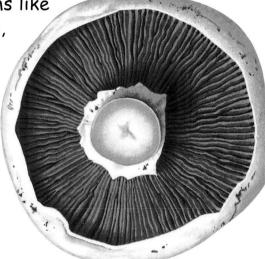

Fungi love warm, damp dark places, such as gaps between toes. If you do not dry your feet, fungi can grow there. Doctors call this infection athlete's foot.

PHONE HOME FACTS

A giant puffball fungus contains seven million million seeds called spores. If each spore grew into a new fungus, all the fungi together would cover an area three times as big as Great Britain.

INFORMATION OVERLOAD!

E.T. has collected so many fascinating facts that he must send them back to his planet to be analysed.

Nearly 2,000 years ago, the wife of Roman emperor Claudius murdered her husband by feeding him a death cap fungi stew.

Black truffle fungi are one of the world's most costly foods. Truffle collectors dig them up from the ground with help from trained pigs.

Bakers use a fungus called yeast to make bread rise. As the yeast grows, it makes bubbles. They produce holes in the loaf, making it lighter.

 21

Plant Defences

E.T. never scrambles with brambles! He knows brambles and nettles are the fighters of the plant world. Their weapons are spikes and stings. Plants use them to stop animals from eating their leaves.

You may feel a stinging nettle before you see it! You can soothe the pain that it causes by rubbing your skin with a dock leaf or baking soda.

Poisonous plant

The milkweed plant contains a poison, but Monarch butterfly caterpillars still eat it. They can because they have poison-proof guts. The weed makes the caterpillars taste bitter. Their bright markings warn birds not to eat them.

If you touch the hairs on stinging nettle leaves, they break off and inject an itchy chemical into your skin.

Prickly problems

Wild blackberries are delicious to eat – but the thorns on blackberry plants scratch fruit-pickers badly! Thorns, spikes and prickles do not just defend a plant's leaves. They also help it to grip other plants so that its shoots can climb and spread.

Thistle prickles do not give the plant total protection. Goats have tough enough mouths to eat the leaves whole.

INFORMATION OVERLOAD!

E.T. has collected so many fascinating facts that he must send them back to his planet to be analysed.

The hairs of stinging plants are shaped like the needles that doctors use to inject medicines through the skin.

People in Java, Indonesia, once believed that the poisonous upas tree made birds flying over it drop dead.

Instead of using wire to keep animals on their land, some Greek farmers put thorn bushes on top of their walls.

23

Growing Great Plants

E.T. finds it difficult to spot spinach or recognize radishes. In the wild, these and other food plants are often tiny, tough and hard to find. People grow them much bigger and better on farms, where they are called crops. To get good results, farmers must prepare the soil and water the plants very carefully.

In hilly places like parts of China there is not enough flat land for growing food. So local farmers plant their crops on terraces – steps cut into the slopes of hills.

Farm machines

Farmers use many machines. Tractors pull ploughs to dig the soil. Seed drills make holes for seeds, then plant them. Combine harvesters cut wheat and separate the seeds we eat from the stalks we do not.

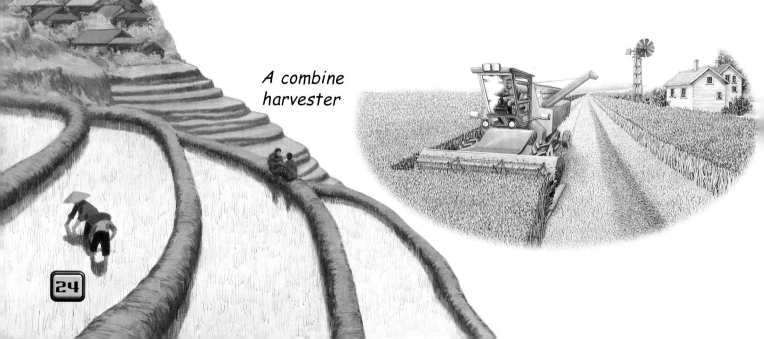

A combine harvester

The Eden Project

At the Eden Project in southwest England, people grow coffee, rubber and other crops from warmer countries in huge plastic domes. Cool-climate crops such as wheat and sunflowers grow out of doors at this exciting new show garden.

Pests such as beetles, slugs and snails find crops as tasty as we do. Ordinary farmers use sprays to kill them. Organic farmers rely on birds, toads and other animals to eat the pests.

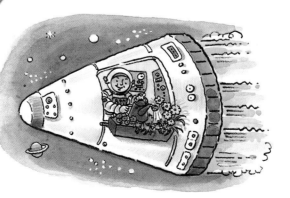

On long space flights in the future, astronauts will have to grow their own food.

INFORMATION OVERLOAD!

E.T. has collected so many fascinating facts that he must send them back to his planet to be analysed.

People probably started farming about 11,000 years ago. Before that, they just gathered wild plants to eat.

By growing seeds from only the best and biggest strawberries, farmers have made their crops 100 times heavier than the wild fruit.

Almost all of our vegetable food comes from only 30 different kinds of food crops.

Plants for Food and Healing

You can walk in a chocolate forest in West Africa. And near your home there may be an aspirin tree growing. Most of the food that people and E.T. eat comes from plants. So do the medicines that make us well.

CHEMIST

Plant medicines are popular because they seem more natural and gentle than doctors' pills. Eating dandelion plants helps speed the flow of water through the body.

Plants that heal

People have always used plants to make themselves well. This foxglove plant is poisonous, but in small amounts, the chemicals in its leaves help weak hearts to beat more strongly. Willow trees can cure headaches. We use their bark to make aspirin tablets.

Do NOT pick foxgloves. They are very dangerous.

EARTH ALERT!
Rainforests are a source of healing plants. If we carry on cutting down forests, we may lose plant cures.

Plant juice

We make most of our drinks from plants – some drinks contain lots! Beer is made from barley. Hops make the drink bitter, yeast makes it fizzy and seaweed keeps it frothy.

Chocolate trees

The cacao (cocoa) beans from which we make chocolate grow on trees. The 'beans' are seeds. They grow in fruit pods. Cacao trees grow in hot, wet places such as West Africa.

COCOA PODS

We would all soon starve without food plants such as wheat, potatoes, fruit and tomatoes. Food animals also eat plants, so without these crops there would be no meat, milk, fish or eggs.

INFORMATION OVERLOAD!

E.T. has collected so many fascinating facts that he must send them back to his planet to be analysed.

We make two very popular drinks – tea and coffee – from plants that were unknown in Europe 400 years ago.

Salt is the only thing we eat that does not rely on plants. People dig it from the ground, or make it by drying out seawater.

About half of all the medicines that people use today began as natural plant cures.

Useful Plants

E.T. cannot imagine a world without wood, cotton or paper. We make all these things from plants. Around the world, 1,000 million people also burn trees to keep warm and to cook.

Tree houses

In some countries, people build whole houses from wood. But even if you live in a brick house, there is wood in it. Wood frames keep the roof up, and hold the glass in the windows.

To make the pages for books, machines called paper mills tear and cook wood into a slushy pulp. When it is spread on to a sieve, the pulp forms sheets of paper.

EARTH ALERT!

Burning wood is better for the planet than burning coal and oil — as long as we replace the trees. Burning any fuel adds harmful gas to the air, but trees absorb it when they regrow.

We get a natural glue called gum arabic from the sap of acacia trees in the African country of Sudan. It is used to seal envelopes and even thicken yoghurt.

Cool clothes

The seeds of cotton plants are fixed to fluffy fibres. Twisting and criss-crossing the fibres makes fabric for jeans and other clothes.

Cotton clothes start with these fluffy seed heads.

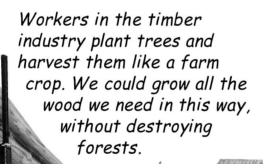

Workers in the timber industry plant trees and harvest them like a farm crop. We could grow all the wood we need in this way, without destroying forests.

INFORMATION OVERLOAD!

E.T. has collected so many fascinating facts that he must send them back to his planet to be analysed.

In the world's poorest countries, trees and other plants supply a third of all the fuel that people burn.

Every year, each European uses about three times their own weight of paper. Each American uses four-and-a-half times their own weight.

Plants are useful to us even when they are still growing. For example, tree roots hold soil in place, helping to stop dangerous landslides.

GOING HOME

E.T. has found out all he needs to know about Plants and now he is ready to go home. Help him get back to his spaceship.

40 Twirl down to 39 on a sycamore seed.	41	42 Bees pollinate your plants. Move to 45.	43
39	38	37 Stop to plant rice. Miss a turn.	36 Where do baby apes sleep? In apricots!	Smell raffles and fa Miss a
20 Build a wooden bridge across to 23.	21	22	23	
19	18 Beetles eat the leaves in your garden. Go back 4 spaces.	17	16	Stop choco Miss
START	1 You wait for your seeds to grow. Miss a turn.	2	3 Climb a giant redwood tree. Move up to 16.	You g athlet Go ba 2 spa

7 | Travel on a puffball spore to 46. **45** | **46** | **47** Float down to 32 on falling autumn leaves. | **48** | **BLAST OFF !**

5 | **34** | **33** | **32** | **31** | **30**

4 | Walk to 29 on giant water lily pads. **25** | **26** | **27** | Slither down some **28** seaweed to 11. | **29**

5 a ar. | **14** | **13** | What's brown and sticky? A stick. **12** | **11** | **10**

4 | **5** | **6** | Sit on a prickly thistle and jump right up to 27. **7** | **8** | Climb up bamboo canes to 30. **9**

Index

astronauts 19, 25
athlete's foot 21

bamboo 7, 14
baobab tree 15
beans 10-11
bees 9
birds 11
blackberries 23
blanket weed 19
bonsai 13
bristlecone pines 5
broadleaf trees 12

cacti 15, 16-17
carbon dioxide 7
century plant 16
cherry tree 9
chlorophyll 7
chocolate 27
coconuts 10
cotton 29
crops 24-25, 27
cycad palms 5

dandelions 26
death cap fungi 20, 21
defences 22-23
desert plants 16-17
drinks 27
duckweed 19

Eden Project 25
evergreen trees 12, 13

farming 24, 25
ferns 5
flowers 5, 8-9, 15
fly agaric mushroom 20
food 4, 24-25, 27
forests 12-13
foxgloves 26
fruits 10
fungi 20-21

glue 29

hay fever 9
honey 9
hot-lips plant 15

insect-eaters 14, 15
insects 8-9

largest flowers 15
leaves 6, 7, 12
lilies 8
living stones 16

medicines 26, 27
milkweed 22
mosses 4
mould 20
mushrooms 20, 21

nectar 9, 17
nettles 22
nuts 10

oaks 12, 13
oldest plants 5
orchids 11
oxygen 4, 7, 12
paper 28, 29
peaches 10
pests 25

pines 5, 12
pitcher plant 14
plankton 18, 19
pollen 8, 9, 17
prickles 23
puffball fungus 21

rafflesias 15
rainforest 5, 12, 13, 26
redwoods 4, 13
roots 7, 17, 29

seaweed 18, 27
seeds 6, 8, 10-11
spruces 13
stamens 8
stinging plants 22, 23
strawberries 25
sundew 15
sunflowers 7
sycamore seeds 11

tallest trees 4, 13
thistles 23
thorns 23
trees 4, 5, 9, 12-13
truffles 21

Venus flytrap 15
vines 7

water lilies 14, 19
water plants 18-19
water weed 18
wild flowers 9
willow trees 26
wood 4, 12, 28, 29

yeast 21, 27

IMAGES: Every effort has been made to trace the copyright holders of the images in this book. The publishers would be pleased to insert appropriate acknowledgments in any subsequent editions of this publication.